Published by

Lion Hudson Limited

Wilkinson House, Jordan Hill Business Park
Banbury Road, Oxford OX2 8DR, England
www.lionhudson.com

ISBN 9780745977942

First edition 2019

A catalogue record for this book is available from the British Library

Printed and bound in China, May 2019, LH54

Albert and the Slingshot

The Story of David and Goliath

Written by Richard Littledale

Illustrated by Heather Heyworth

LION
CHILDREN'S

Albert and all the little mice were gathered at the edge of the field. The sun was high in the sky, and each mouse was nestling under a leafy branch like their own personal sunshade.

"We love it here," one of them said. "We feel so much safer here than in the barn."

"Hmm," said Albert. "Did I ever tell you the story of the slingshot?"

Every little pair of tufty ears flapped this way and that as they shook their heads.

"When he was young, my great-great-great-uncle
Barney loved being out in the fields, too," said Albert.
"He used to scamper around the sheep.

"If a lion or wolf came too close,
he'd tuck himself inside the bag
of a shepherd boy named David.
David would always fight them off.

"One day, David's dad gave him a job to do.

"'Take this basket of food and drink to your brothers at the battlefront,' he said.

"David didn't really want to go, as he knew his brothers would tease him, but to please his dad, off he went.

"That was when Barney made his big mistake," said Albert gravely.

"Whatever did he do?" squeaked Lucy, a small wide-eyed mouse.

"He climbed into the basket," said Albert. "As David took each step, poor Barney was joggled from side to side.

"When the walking stopped, Barney peeked over the basket to see what was happening outside."

"Was there a terrible battle going on?" roared Smokey, a grey mouse with a very loud voice.

"No," said Albert, "the whole army were just standing about. Well, in fact they weren't so much standing about, as hiding and crouching down low.

"David asked them what was going on. At last, one of them told him, 'He's the problem,' and jabbed a thumb up over the grassy bank where they were hiding.

"Barney was wondering who the man meant when a mighty roar split the air. It rattled the branches of the trees, and made the clay bottles in the basket clink together, so hard that they almost squashed him. Barney wriggled out and into the safety of David's bag.

"'Come on you cowards,' the giant Goliath roared. 'What's the matter with you? Send a champion out to fight me and we'll soon see who's the boss around here.'

"David looked around to see who would answer. Why are they frightened of a silly old giant, he thought, when they've got God on their side? David waited and waited, but nobody said a thing.

"David started asking anyone he could see, 'Why don't you fight him?'

"The king himself got to hear of it and sent for David.

"'Please, Your Majesty,' David said in a squeaky voice, 'let me go and fight him, Sire.'

"'You?' said the king, the silver armour on his belly jangling up and down as he laughed at the very idea.

'Yes, Sire!' said David. 'God kept me safe from lions and wolves, so why can't he keep me safe from this giant?'

"The king could see that David's mind was made up, so he told him, 'Go! I pray that God will keep you safe.'

"The king placed his armour on David, and it came all the way down to his toes. He put his heavy helmet on his head, and David could hardly lift it. When he strapped on his sword and tried to take a step, he tripped right over with a

SPLAT!

"'I'm sorry, Your Majesty,'
David said, 'but I just
can't wear all this.'

"Leaving the armour behind, David picked his way down the grassy bank to a sparkly stream that flowed nearby. Bending down he picked up one, two, three, four, five stones, dried them off on his tunic, and put them in his bag. With each one, Barney had to dodge this way and that as they came rattling down. Then David walked out to face the giant.

"'Ho ho ho!' roared the giant, the ground shaking with every 'ho'. 'What kind of joke is this, boy? Take one step closer and I'll break you up and feed you to the birds.'

"David wasn't frightened. 'I'm not scared of you,' shouted David across the battlefield. 'God is with me, and you're the one who'll end up broken.'

"The ground began to shake with a

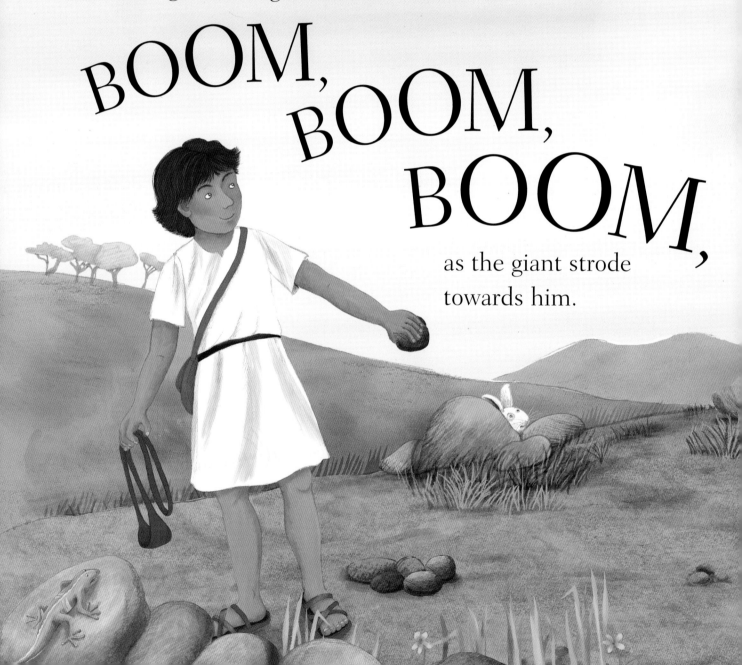

BOOM, BOOM, BOOM,

as the giant strode towards him.

"At that moment, David's hand shot down into the bag. His fingers pushed past Barney's furry back, just missing him as they closed around a stone. He loaded it into his sling and let go.

"'Phew!' said Barney, deep down in the bag.

WHOOOSH, went the air, as the stone rushed through it.

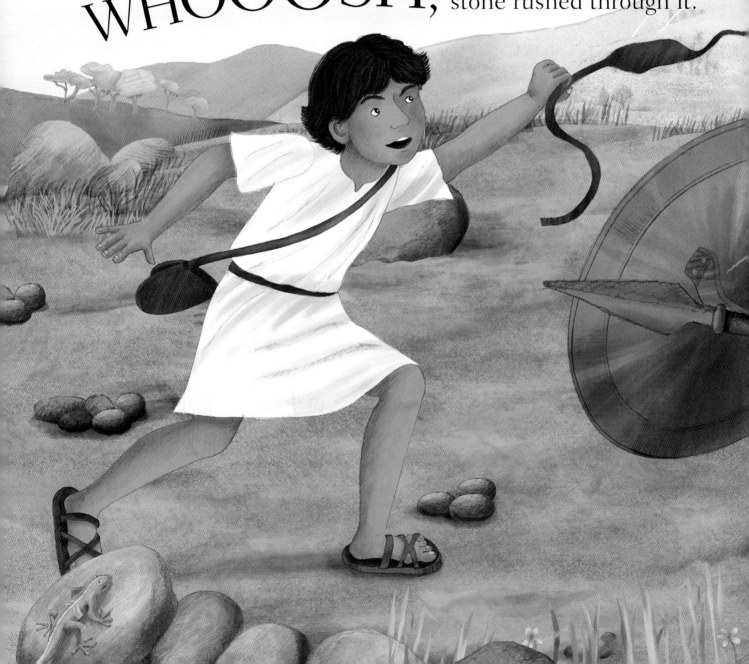

THUNK, went the stone as it hit the giant Goliath right on his big ugly head.

KERRASH, went everything, as the giant fell down on the battlefield.

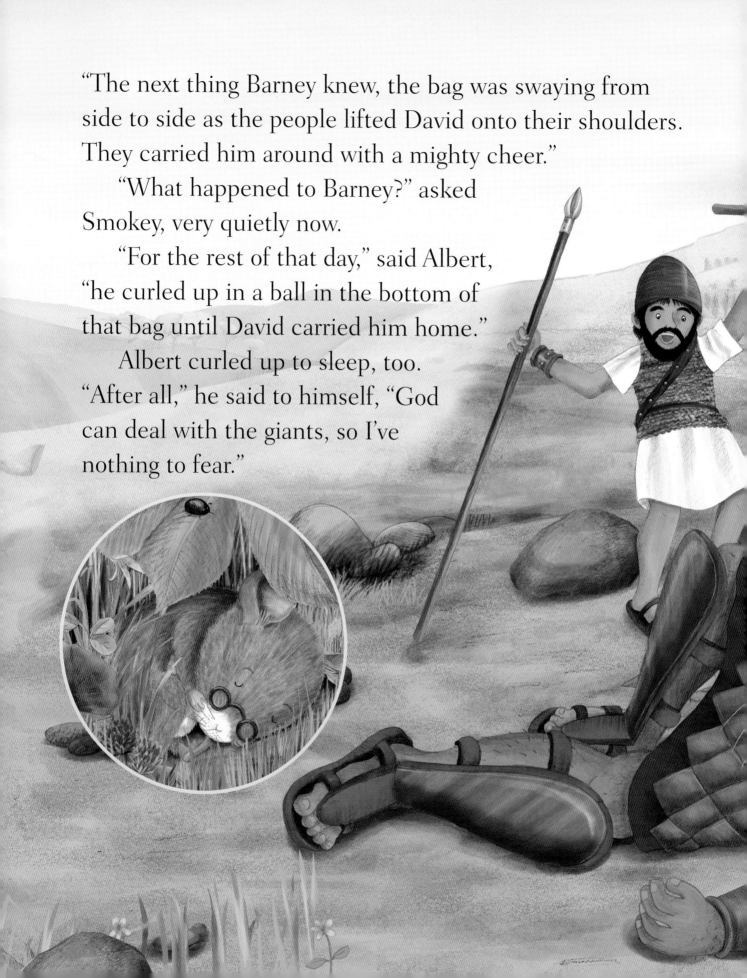

"The next thing Barney knew, the bag was swaying from side to side as the people lifted David onto their shoulders. They carried him around with a mighty cheer."

"What happened to Barney?" asked Smokey, very quietly now.

"For the rest of that day," said Albert, "he curled up in a ball in the bottom of that bag until David carried him home."

Albert curled up to sleep, too. "After all," he said to himself, "God can deal with the giants, so I've nothing to fear."